YUMMY Keto Chaffl

Quick and Super Easy Low Carb Recipes for Delicious Waffles to Maintain Your Ketogenic Diet and Lose Weight!

BY

BRENDA GREY

Contents

INTRODUCTION TO CHAFFELS

A chaffle is a delicious dish made with eggs, melty cheddar and seasonings joined and prepared in a chaff producer, to make crunchy, low carb chaff.

How much time does it take to make chaff?

A chaffle can take somewhere in the range of 5-10 minutes to make contingent upon your chaff producer and what a number of you're making.

What sorts of cheddar would I be able to use in chaff?

You need to be sure the cheddar you're utilizing can dissolve, but at the same time is tight. I prescribe cheeses like cheddar and mozzarella as a beginning stage.

Would you be able to make chaffles ahead?

Truly! You can make bunches early and freeze them for as long as seven days. Warmth them in your toaster, or by enveloping them by a soaked towel and microwaving for 20-30 seconds. Note: sweet chaffle plans wind up tasting gooey again when re-warmed, so you may need to include a scramble of cinnamon, or some keto-accommodating sugar after it's warmed.

Here's the intriguing thing about this
although the chaff contains no grains,
the base of this Keto chaff is cheddar.

- What's more, I realize you see this like, "did this lady extremely simply state cheddar?"
- Indeed – the most excellent stabilizer right now is mozzarella cheddar.

CRISPY CHAFFLE

PREPARATION TIME: 5 minutes

COOKING TIME: 5 minutes

TOTAL TIME: 10 minutes

SERVINGS: 2

INGREDIENTS

- 2 eggs

- 1/2 cup parmesan cheese

- Everything except 1 teaspoon bagel

- 1/2 cup mozzarella cheese

- 2 teaspoon almond flour

PREPARATIONS

1. Heat the mini waffle maker for about 30 seconds. Sprinkle the griddle with a range of cheese (I used Parmesan and Mozzarella cheese), melt and bake for 30 seconds, then add the mixture.

2. In a small bowl, add 2 eggs, 1 cup of cheese, 2 teaspoons of almond flour and bagel seasoning (if you are not a fan, you can skip the seasoning) and whisk.

3. Pour the mixture into a waffle maker so that it does not spill from the bottom.

4. Cook for 4 minutes (the longer the

14

cooking time, the quicker the crisper).

5. This mixture has two chaffles.

NUTRITIONAL VALUE

Yield: 2 servings, 1 serving: 1 crispy shuffle

Serving Size: Calories: 287, Total Carbohydrates: 6g, Fiber: 0g, Net Carbohydrates: 6g, Total Fat: 20g, Protein: 21g

ORIGINAL CHAFFLE

PREPARATION TIME: 5 minutes

COOKING TIME: 5 minutes

TOTAL TIME: 10 minutes

SERVINGS: 1

INGREDIENTS

- 2 eggs
- 1 cup cheddar cheese

PREPARATIONS

1. Heat mini waffle maker (takes 30 seconds).

2. Whisk 2 eggs and 1 cup cheese in a small bowl.

3. Add the mixture to the waffle maker and spell for 2-3 minutes.

4. This mixture makes two chaffles.

NUTRITIONAL VALUE

Yield: 2 servings, 1 serving: 1 oriental chaffle

Serving Size: Calories: 168, Total Carbohydrates: 1g, Fiber: 0g, Net Carbohydrates: 1g, Total Fat: 13g, Protein: 12g

PUMPKIN SPICE CHAFFLE

PREPARATION TIME: 5 minutes

COOKING TIME: 5 minutes

TOTAL TIME: 10 minutes

SERVINGS: 2

INGREDIENTS

- Pumpkin spice shuffle

- 2 eggs
- 2/3 cup mozzarella cheese
- 3 tablespoons of pumpkin puree
- 2 tsp cinnamon
- 2 teaspoons swab
- 3 teaspoons of almond flour

PREPARATIONS

1. Heat mini waffle maker instructions (should take 30 seconds).
2. Whisk in one place all the ingredients.
3. Add half of the waffle maker mixture.
4. Cook for 2 or 3 minutes (the longer you cook the chaffle is going to be the crispier) this blend should make 2 chaffles.
5. Finish with hard (optional) whipped cream.

NUTRITIONAL VALUE

Calories: 218, Total Carbohydrates: 10g, Fiber: 2g, Net Carbohydrates: 6g, Sugar Alcohol: 2g, Total Fat: 15g, Protein: 16g

CINNAMON SUGAR (CHURRO) CHAFFLE:

PREPARATION TIME: 5 minutes

COOKING TIME: 7 minutes

TOTAL TIME: 12 minutes

SERVINGS: 3

INGREDIENTS:

- One large egg

- 3/4 cup mozzarella cheese (shredded)

- 2 tablespoons blanched almond flour (or 2 tsp coconut flour)

- 1/2 tbsp (melted)

- 2 tbsp erythritol

- 1/2 teaspoon of cinnamon

- 1/2 teaspoon of vanilla essence

- 1/2 teaspoon psyllium husk powder (optional, for texture)

- 1/4 teaspoon baking powder (optional)

- 1 tablespoon butter (melted, for toppings)

- Erythritol 1/4 cup (for topping)

- 3/4 teaspoon of cinnamon (for topping)

PREPARATIONS:

1. Heat the iron for about 5 minutes until hot.

2. If your recipe includes cream cheese, put it in a bowl first. Gently heat in a microwave (15-30 seconds) or double boiler until soft and stir.

3. Stir all remaining ingredients (except toppings, if any).

4. Pour a sufficient amount of shuffle dough into the waffle maker and cover the surface firmly. (For a normal waffle maker, about 1/2 cup, for a mini waffle maker, about 1/4 cup.)

5. Cook for about 3-4 minutes until brown and crisp.

6. Carefully remove the shuffle from the waffle maker and set aside for a crisp noise. (Cooling is important for the texture!) If there is any dough, repeat with the remaining dough.

NUTRITION VALUE

- Calories 208

- 16g fat

- 11g protein

- 4g total carbs

- 2g pure carbohydrate

- Fiber2g

- Sugar 0g

GARLIC BREAD CHAFFLE

PREPARATION TIME: 5 minutes

COOKING TIME: 6 minutes

TOTAL TIME: 11 minutes

SERVINGS: 2

INGREDIENTS

- 1/2 cup mozzarella cheese shredded

- 1 egg

- 1 teaspoon Italian seasoning

- 1/2 teaspoon of garlic

- 1 teaspoon cream cheese I like to use flavored cream cheese such as leek, onion, jalapeno, but you can also use plain

- Garlic butter topping ingredient
- 1 tablespoon butter
- 1/2 tsp Italian seasoning
- 1/2 teaspoon of garlic
- Cheesy bread topping
- 2 tbs mozzarella cheese shredded
- Parsley dash or more Italian seasonings

PREPARATIONS

1. Preheat the oven to 350F.

2. Mix all the ingredients of the garlic minced bread until well combined.

3. Divide the mixture in half and cook the first tablespoon for at least 4 minutes. If you like a little crunchy on the outside, I would recommend that you put a tsp of shredded cheese on the waffle maker 30

seconds before adding the ingredients. This is going to make a sweet, crunchy crust that's pretty amazing!

4. After you have cooked both of the garlic bread chops in the waffle maker, move them to the baking sheet.

5. Melt the butter in a separate small bowl in a microwave for about 10 seconds.

6. Apply the seasonings of garlic butter to the butter mixture.

7. Rub the butter mixture over the moist cloves with a basting brush.

8. Sprinkle with a small amount of mozzarella on top of the garlic bread and sprinkle with more Italian seasoning.

9. Bake at 350F degrees for 5 minutes. It's just enough time to melt the cheese on top of the Cheesy Garlic Bread Chaffle!

10. Serve warm and enjoy a sugar-free marinara sauce such as Rao's marinara sauce!

Notes: Please serve warm and enjoy

NUTRITIONAL VALUE

- Calories 220
- Total Fat 10.5g 16%
- Cholesterol 87.2mg   29%
- Sodium 87.3mg   4%
- Total Carbohydrate 9.2g   3%
- Dietary Fiber 1.4g   5%
- Sugars 1.1g
- Protein 4.1g   8%
- Vitamin A 106.8µg   7%
- Vitamin C 0mg   0%

CAKE CHAFFLES

KETO CHOCOLATE WAFFLE CAKE

PREPARATION TIME: 5 minutes

COOKING TIME: 5 minutes

TOTAL TIME: 10 minutes

SERVINGS: 3

INGREDIENTS

- 2 Tbs cocoa

- 2 Tbs Monkfruit Confectioner's

- 1 egg

- 1/4 teaspoon baking powder

- 1 Tbs Heavy Whipped Cream

Frosted ingredients

- 2 Tbs Monkfruit Confectioners

- 2 Tbs cream cheese softens, room temperature

- 1/4 teaspoon transparent vanilla

PREPARATIONS

1. Whip the egg in a small bowl.

2. Add other ingredients and mix well until smooth and creamy.

3. Cook until fully cooked for 2 1/2 to 3

minutes.

4. Add the sweetener, cream cheese, and vanilla in a separate small bowl. Mix the frosting until all is well embedded.

5. Spread the frosting after it has cooled down to room temperature.

NUTRITIONAL VALUE

- Calories   120
- Total Fat 10.5g   16%
- Cholesterol 87.2mg   29%
- Sodium 87.3mg   4%
- Total Carbohydrate 9.2g   3%
- Dietary Fiber 1.4g   5%
- Sugars 1.1g
- Protein 4.1g   8%
- Vitamin A 106.8μg   7%
- Vitamin C 0mg   0%

KETO BIRTHDAY CAKE CHAFFLE RECIPE WITH SPRINKLES

PREPARATION TIME: 10 minutes

COOKING TIME: 7 minutes

TOTAL TIME: 17 minutes

SERVINGS: 4

INGREDIENTS:
Ingredients for shuffle cake:

- 2 eggs

- 1/4 almond flour

- 1 cup of coconut powder

- 1 cup melted butter

- 2 tablespoons cream cheese

- 1 teaspoon cake butter extract

- 1 tsp vanilla extract

- 2 tsp baking powder

- 2 teaspoons confectionery sweetener or monk fruit

- 1/4 teaspoon xanthan powder whipped cream

vanilla frosting Ingredients:

- 1/2 cup heavy whipped cream
- 2 tablespoons sweetener or monk fruit
- 1/2 teaspoon vanilla extract

PREPARATIONS:

1. The mini waffle maker is preheated.

2. Add all the ingredients of the chaffle cake in a medium-sized blender and blend it to the top until it is smooth and creamy. Allow only a minute to sit with the batter. It may seem a little watery, but it's going to work well.

3. Add 2 to 3 tablespoons of batter to your waffle maker and cook until golden brown for about 2 to 3 minutes.

4. Start to frost the whipped vanilla cream in a separate bowl.

5. Add all the ingredients and mix with a hand mixer until the whipping cream forms thick and soft peaks.

6. Until frosting your cake, allow the keto birthday cake chaffles to cool completely. If you frost it

too soon, the frosting will be melted.

7. Enjoy! Enjoy!

Notes (makes four mini cakes)

NUTRITIONAL VALUE

- Calories 141
- Total Fat 10.2g   16%
- Cholesterol 111mg   37%
- Sodium 55.7mg   2%
- Total Carbohydrate 4.7g   2%
- Dietary Fiber 0.4g   2%
- Sugars 0.8g
- Protein 4.7g   9%
- Vitamin A 96.6μg   6%
- Vitamin C 0mg   0%

CARROT CHAFFLE CAKE

PREPARATION TIME: 5 minutes

COOKING TIME: 5 minutes

TOTAL TIME: 10 minutes

SERVINGS: 6

INGREDIENTS

- 1/2 cup chopped carrot

- 1 egg

- 2 T butter melted

- 2 T heavy whipped cream

- 3/4 cup almond flour

- 1 walnut chopped

- 2 T powder sweetener

- 2 tsp cinnamon

- 1 tsp pumpkin spice

- 1 tsp baking powder

- Cream cheese frosting

- 4 oz cream cheese softened

- 1/4 cup powdered sweetener

- 1 teaspoon of vanilla essence

- 1-2 T heavy whipped cream according to your preferred consistency

PREPARATIONS

1. Mix dry ingredients such as almond flour, cinnamon, pumpkin spices, baking powder, powdered sweeteners, and walnut pieces.

2. Add the grated carrots, eggs, melted butter and cream.

3. Add a 3T batter to a preheated mini waffle maker. Cook for 2 1 / 2-3 minutes.

4. Mix the frosted ingredients with a hand mixer with a whisk until well mixed

5. Stack waffles and add a frost between each layer!

Note

(Serving) 2.4 non-freezing net carbohydrates, 3.7 net carbs with icing, 1/4 of the cake are 5.5 net carbs!

NUTRITIONAL VALUE

KETO VANILLA TWINKIE COPYCAT CHAFFLE

PREPARATION TIME: 5 minutes

COOKING TIME: 4 minutes

TOTAL TIME: 9 minutes

SERVINGS: 4

INGREDIENTS

- 2 tablespoons of butter (cooled)

- 2 oz cream cheese softened

- Two large egg room temperature

- 1 teaspoon of vanilla essence

- Optional 1/2 teaspoon vanilla cupcake extract

- 1/4 cup Lacanto confectionery

- Pinch of salt

- 1/4 cup almond flour

- 2 tablespoons coconut powder

- 1 teaspoon baking powder

PREPARATIONS

1. Preheat Corndog Maker.

2. Melt the butter and let cool for 1 minute.

3. Whisk the butter until the eggs are creamy.

4. Add vanilla, extract, sweetener and salt and mix well.

5. Add almond flour, coconut flour, baking powder.

6. Mix until well incorporated.

7. Add ~ 2 tbs batter to each well and spread evenly.

8. Close and lock the lid and cook for 4 minutes.

9. Remove and cool the rack.

NUTRITIONAL VALUE

- Calories   152
- Total Fat 9g   14%
- Cholesterol 100.7mg 34%
- Sodium 727.7mg   30%
- Total Carbohydrate 6.5g   2%
- Dietary Fiber 1.6g   6%
- Sugars 2.4g
- Protein 6.1g   12%
- Vitamin A 120.2µg   8%
- Vitamin C 0mg   0%

BANANA PUDDING CHAFFLE CAKE

PREPARATION TIME: 5 minutes

COOKING TIME: 5 minutes

TOTAL TIME: 10 minutes

SERVINGS: 2

INGREDIENTS

- 1 large egg yolk
- 1/2 cup fresh cream
- 3 T powder sweetener
- 1 / 4-1 / 2 teaspoon xanthan gum
- 1/2 teaspoon banana extract
- Banana chaffle ingredients
- 1 oz softened cream cheese
- 1/4 cup mozzarella cheese shredded
- 1 egg

- 1 teaspoon banana extract

- 2 T sweetener

- 1 tsp baking powder

- 4 T almond flour

PREPARATIONS

1. Mix heavy cream, powdered sweetener and egg yolk in a small pot. Whisk constantly until the sweetener has dissolved and the mixture is thick.

2. Cook for 1 minute. Add xanthan gum and whisk.

3. Remove from heat, add a pinch of salt and banana extract and stir well.

4. Transfer to a glass dish and cover the pudding with plastic wrap. Refrigerate.

5. Mix all ingredients together. Cook in a preheated mini waffle maker.

6. Note

7. Make three shuffles. 3.3 Net carbs/serving. Recipe 9.8 Net carbs

NUTRITIONAL VALUE

EASY SOFT CINNAMON ROLLS CHAFFLE CAKE

PREPARATION TIME: 5 minutes

COOKING TIME: 12 minutes

TOTAL TIME: 17 minutes

SERVINGS: 3

INGREDIENTS

- 1 egg
- 1/2 cup mozzarella cheese
- 1/2 tsp vanilla
- 1/2 tsp cinnamon
- 1 tbs monk fruit confectioners blend

PREPARATION

1. Put the eggs in a small bowl.

2. Add the remaining ingredients.

3. Spray to the waffle maker with a non-stick cooking spray.

4. Make two shuffles.

5. Separate the mixture.

6. Cook half of the mixture for about 4 minutes or until golden.

Notes Added Glaze: 1 tb of cream cheese melted in a microwave for 15 seconds, and 1 tb of monk fruit confectioners mix. Mix it and spread it over the moist fabric.

Additional Frosting: 1 tb cream cheese (high temp), 1 tb room temp butter (low temp) and 1 tb monk fruit confectioners' mix. Mix all the ingredients together and spread to the top of the cloth.

Top with optional frosting, glaze, nuts, sugar-free syrup, whipped cream or simply dust with monk fruit sweets.

NUTRITIONAL VALUE

- Calories   106

- Total Fat 6.6g 10%

- Cholesterol 107mg   36%

- Sodium 182.3mg   8%

- Total Carbohydrate 4.6g   2%

- Dietary Fiber 0.3g   1%

- Sugars 2.7g

- Protein 8.2g   16%

- Vitamin A 94.7µg   6%

- Vitamin C 0mg   0%

KETO ITALIAN CREAM CHAFFLE CAKE

PREPARATION TIME: 5 minutes

COOKING TIME: 3 minutes

TOTAL TIME: 8 minutes

SERVINGS: 1

INGREDIENTS

For sweet shuffle:

- 4 oz cream cheese softens, room temperature
- 4 eggs
- 1 tablespoon butter
- 1 teaspoon of vanilla essence
- 1/2 teaspoon of cinnamon
- 1 tbsp monk fruit sweetener or favorite keto-approved sweetener
- 4 tablespoons coconut powder
- 1 tablespoon almond flour
- 1 1/2 cup baking powder
- 1 tablespoon coconut
- 1 walnut chopped
- Italian cream frosting ingredients:
- 2 oz. Cream cheese softens, room temperature
- 2 cups of butter room temp
- 2 tbs monk fruit sweetener or favorite keto-

approved sweetener

- 1/2 teaspoon vanilla

PREPARATIONS

1. In a medium blender, add cream cheese, eggs, melted butter, vanilla, sweeteners, coconut flour, almond flour, and baking powder. Optional: Add shredded coconut and walnut to the mixture or save for matting. Both methods are great!

2. Mix the ingredients high until smooth and creamy.

3. Preheat mini waffle maker.

4. Add ingredients to the preheated waffle maker.

5. Cook for about 2-3 minutes until the waffle is complete.

6. Remove shuffle and let cool.

7. In a separate bowl, add all the ingredients together and start frosting. Stir until smooth and creamy.

8. When the shuffle has cooled completely, frost

the cake.

Note

Create 8 mini shuffles or 3-4 large shuffles.

NUTRITIONAL VALUE

- Calories   127
- % Daily Value*
- Total Fat 9.7g 15%
- Cholesterol 102.9mg   34%
- Sodium 107.3mg   4%
- Total Carbohydrate 5.5g   2%
- Dietary Fiber 1.3g   5%
- Sugars 1.5g
- Protein 5.3g   11%
- Vitamin A 99µg   7%
- Vitamin C 0.1mg   0%

KETO PEANUT BUTTER CHAFFLE

CAKE

PREPARATION TIME: 5 minutes

COOKING TIME: 5 minutes

TOTAL TIME: 10 minutes

SERVINGS: 2

INGREDIENTS

Ingredients for peanut butter shuffle:

- 2 Tbs Sugar-Free Peanut Butter Powder

- 2 Tbs Monkfruit Confectioner's

- 1 egg

- 1/4 teaspoon baking powder

- 1 Tbs Heavy Whipped Cream

- 1/4 teaspoon peanut butter extract

Peanut butter frosting ingredients

- 2 Tbs Monkfruit Confectioners

- 1 Tbs butter softens, room temperature

- 1 tbs unsweetened natural peanut butter or peanut butter powder

- 2 Tbs cream cheese softens, room temperature

- 1/4 tsp vanilla

PREPARATIONS

1. Serve the eggs in a small bowl.

2. Add the ingredients and mix well until the dough is smooth and creamy.

3. If you don't have peanut butter extract, you can skip it. It adds absolutely

wonderful, more powerful peanut butter flavor and is worth investing in this extract.

4. Pour half of the butter into a mini waffle maker and cook for 2-3 minutes until it is completely cooked.

5. In another small bowl, add sweetener, cream cheese, sugar-free natural peanut butter and vanilla. Mix frosting until everything is well incorporated.

6. When the waffle cake has completely cooled to room temperature, spread the frosting.

7. Or you can even pipe the frost!

8. Or you can heat the frosting and add 1/2 teaspoon of water to make the peanut butter aze pill and drizzle over the peanut butter chaffle! I like it anyway!

NUTRITIONAL VALUE

- Calories   92
- Total Fat 7g   11%
- Cholesterol 97.1mg   32%
- Sodium 64.3mg   3%
- Total Carbohydrate 3.6g   1%
- Dietary Fiber 0.6g   3%
- Sugars 1.8g
- Protein 5.5g   11%
- Vitamin A 52.1µg   3%
- Vitamin C 0mg   0%

KETO BIRTHDAY CAKE CHAFFLE

PREPARATION TIME: 10 minutes

COOKING TIME: 5 minutes

TOTAL TIME: 15 minutes

SERVINGS: 4

INGREDIENTS

Ingredients for shuffle cake:

- 2 eggs

- 1/4 cup almond flour

- Coconut flower 1 teaspoon

- 2 tablespoons of melted butter

- 2 tablespoons of cream cheese

- 1 teaspoon cake batter extract

- 1/2 teaspoon of vanilla essence

- 1/2 teaspoon baking powder

- 2 tablespoons sweetener or monk fruit

- 1/4 teaspoon xanthan powder

Whipped cream vanilla frosting ingredients:

- 1/2 cup fresh cream

- 2 tablespoons sweets sweetener or monk fruit

- 1/2 teaspoon of vanilla essence

PREPARATIONS

1. Preheat mini waffle maker.

2. In a medium-sized blender, add all the ingredients of the shuffle cake and blend high until smooth and creamy. Let the dough sit for only one minute. It may look a bit watery, but it works.

3. Add 2-3 tablespoons of dough to the waffle maker and cook for about 2-3 minutes until golden.

4. In another bowl, start making the whipped cream vanilla frosting.

5. Add all ingredients and mix them well until whipped cream thickens and soft peaks form.

6. Let the keto birthday cake chaffle cool completely before frosting the cake. If the frost is too early, the frost will melt.

7. Pleasant!

Note: (Make four mini cakes)

NUTRITIONAL VALUE

- Calories   141

- Total Fat 10.2g   16%

- Cholesterol 111mg   37%

- Sodium 55.7mg   2%

- Total Carbohydrate 4.7g   2%

- Dietary Fiber 0.4g   2%

- Sugars 0.8g

- Protein 4.7g   9%

- Vitamin A 96.6µg   6%

- Vitamin C 0mg   0%

KETO BOSTON CREAM PIE CHAFFLE CAKE

PREPARATION TIME: 10 minutes

COOKING TIME: 5 minutes

TOTAL TIME: 15 minutes

SERVINGS: 4

INGREDIENTS

Ingredients for shuffle cake:

- 2 eggs
- 1/4 cup almond flour
- Coconut flower 1 teaspoon
- 2 tablespoons of melted butter
- 2 tablespoons of cream cheese
- 20 drops of Boston Cream Extract
- 1/2 teaspoon of vanilla essence
- 1/2 teaspoon baking powder
- 2 tablespoons sweetener or monk fruit
- 1/4 teaspoon xanthan powder

Custard Ingredients:

- 1/2 cup fresh cream
- 1/2 teaspoon of vanilla essence
- 1/2 tbs Swerve confectioners Sweetener
- 2 yolks
- 1/8 teaspoon xanthan gum

Ingredients for ganache:

- 2 tbs heavy whipped cream

- 2 tbs unsweetened baking chocolate bar chopped

- 1 tbs Swerve Confectioners sweetener

PREPARATION

1. Preheat the mini waffle iron to render the cake chops first.

2. Mix all the ingredients of the cake and blend until smooth and fluffy. It's only supposed to take a few minutes.

3. Heat the heavy whipping cream to a boil on the stovetop. While it's dry, whisk the egg yolks together in a small separate dish.

4. Once the cream is boiling, add half of it to the egg yolks. Make sure you're whisking it together while you're slowly pouring it into the mixture.

5. Take off from the heat and whisk in your vanilla and xanthan gum. Then set aside to cool and thicken.

6. Place the ganache ingredients in a small bowl. Microwave for about 20 seconds, stir. Repeat, if necessary. Careful not to overheat and roast the ganache. Just do it 20 seconds at a time until it's completely melted.

7. Assemble and enjoy your Boston Cream Pie Chaffle Cake!!

Notes (makes four mini cakes)

KETO CHAFFLE GARLIC BREADSTICKS

PREPARATION TIME: 3 minutes

COOKING TIME: 7 minutes

TOTAL TIME: 10 minutes

SERVINGS: 8

INGREDIENTS

- 1 medium egg
- 1/2 cup of mozzarella cheese grated
- 2 tablespoons almond flour
- 1/2 teaspoon garlic powder
- 1/2 teaspoon oregano
- 1/2 teaspoon salt

TOPPING

- 2 tablespoons butter, salt-free
- 1/2 teaspoon garlic powder
- 1/4 cup mozzarella cheese grated
- US Customs-Metric

PREPARATION

1. Turn on your waffle maker and graze it

slightly (I give you a light olive oil spray) Beat the egg in a bowl.

2. Add the almond flour, mozzarella, garlic powder, oregano and salt and mix well.

3. Spoon the batter into your waffle maker (mine is a square double waffle and this mixture covers both waffle sections. If you use half of the mixture in a smaller waffle maker spoon at a time).

4. I spoon my mixture into my waffle manufacturer's middle and scatter it softly to the bottom.

5. Use tongs to remove the cooked waffles and cut each waffle into 4 strips.

6. Place the sticks on a tray and fire the grill beforehand.

7. Mix the butter with the paste of garlic and scatter over the ends.

8. Sprinkle the mozzarella over the sticks and place 2-3 minutes under the grill until the cheese melts and bubbles.

9. Eat right now! Notes Net carbs will be the total carb count minus the fiber count (even though we've eaten this heated up but are much nicer freshly made). Carb count excludes alcohols from sugar.

10. Any website nutritional analysis is based on an estimate, calculated in each recipe from the individual ingredients. Variations can occur for different reasons, including the availability of goods and the preparation of food. We do not offer any statement or promise that this information is accurate.

NUTRITIONAL VALUE

Calories: 74kcal | Carbohydrates: 0.9g | Protein: 3.4g | Fat: 6.5g | Fiber: 0.2g

KETO LOW CARB CREAM CHEESE MINI WAFFLES

PREPARATION TIME: 5 minutes

COOKING TIME: 8 minutes

TOTAL TIME: 13 minutes

SERVINGS: 4

INGREDIENTS

PREPARATION

NUTRITIONAL VALUE

KETO BLUEBERRY CHAFFLE

PREPARATION TIME: 3 minutes

COOKING TIME: 10 minutes

TOTAL TIME: 13 minutes

SERVINGS:

INGREDIENTS

- Mozzarella cheese shredded
- 3 tablespoons almond flour
- 2 eggs
- 2 teaspoons
- 1 tsp cinnamon
- 1/2 teaspoon baking powder
- 1/2 cup fresh blueberry
- 1/2 teaspoon of powder swab (optional)

PREPARATION

1. Start with the waffle maker's heating.

2. Start shuffling with mozzarella cheese, almond flour, eggs, sweetener, cinnamon, baking powder and vanilla extract.

3. Stir the blueberries gently once the ingredients are well mixed. Do not use frozen blueberries, as the extra moisture makes the shuffle less crispy.

4. Open the cover and cook.

5. After cooking for about 8 minutes, start checking for chaffle. Open the waffle maker carefully. Open and cook for another minute or two when shuffles start to fall apart. This is done when crispy, allowing you to open the waffle maker without pulling the shuffle.

6. To provide a shuffle: sprinkle a small amount of powdered swab over the top of the shuffle. Enjoy your favorite sugar and drizzle-free, keto-friendly syrup!

NUTRITIONAL VALUE

- Calories 193

- Total Fat 12g

- Sodium 325mg

- Carbohydrates 9g

- Net Carbohydrates 3g

- Fiber 2g

- Sugar Alcohols 4g

- Protein 13g

MAPLE PUMPKIN KETO CHAFFLE

PREPARATION TIME: 5 minutes

COOKING TIME: 8 minutes

TOTAL TIME: 13 minutes

SERVINGS: 4

INGREDIENTS

PREPARATION

NUTRITIONAL VALUE

CHAFFLE

PREPARATION TIME: 5 minutes

COOKING TIME: 8 minutes

TOTAL TIME: 13 minutes

SERVINGS: 4

INGREDIENTS

PREPARATION

NUTRITIONAL VALUE

KRISPY KREME COPYCAT OF THE GLAZED RASPBERRY JELLY-FILLED DONUT

PREPARATION TIME: 5 minutes

COOKING TIME: 8 minutes

TOTAL TIME: 13 minutes

SERVINGS: 4

INGREDIENTS

- 1 egg

- 1/4 cup mozzarella cheese shredded

- 2 T cream cheese softening

- 1 T sweetener

- 1 T almond powder

- 1/2 teaspoon baking powder

- 20 drops of glazed donut flavor

Raspberry jelly filling ingredients

- Raspberry cup 1/4

- 1 teaspoon chia seed

- 1 tsp sugar confectionery

- Donut Gla Medicine Ingredients

- 1 teaspoon of powdered sweetener

- A few drops of water or cream

PREPARATIONS

1. Create a shuffle.
2. Mix everything and make the shuffle first.
3. Cook for about 2 1/2 minutes.
4. Make a raspberry jelly filling:
5. Stir in a small pan over medium heat.

6. Gently mash the raspberry.

7. Let cool.

8. Add between layers of shuffle.

9. Make Donut Gla Medicine:

10. Stir together in a small dish.

11. Shuffle drizzle on top.

Note

Make three shuffles. 1.5 net carbs each, With jam and glaze, the entire recipe contains 6.5 pure carbs.

NUTRITIONAL VALUE

- Calories   150
- Total Fat 11.2g 17%
- Cholesterol 113.3mg   38%
- Sodium 96.9mg   4%
- Total Carbohydrate 5.9g   2%
- Dietary Fiber 1.7g   7%

- Sugars 2.7g

- Protein 4.6g   9%

- Vitamin A 104μg   7%

- Vitamin C 0mg   0%

JICAMA HASH BROWN CHAFFLE

PREPARATION TIME: 5 minutes

COOKING TIME: 8 minutes

TOTAL TIME: 13 minutes

SERVINGS: 2

INGREDIENTS

- 1 large jicama root
- 1/2 onion chopped
- 2 garlic
- I used the 1 cup Haloumi that I chose
- 2 eggs
- Salt and pepper

PREPARATIONS

1. Skin Jicama
2. Shred with food processor
3. Put the shredded jig in a large colander and sprinkle
4. 1-2 teaspoon salt, Mix well and drain.
5. 5-8 minutes microwave oven
6. Mix all ingredients together
7. Add 3T mixture and sprinkle a little more

cheese

8. On the mixture

NUTRITIONAL VALUE

- Calories 168

- Total Fat 11.8g 18%

- Cholesterol 121mg   40%

- Sodium 221.8mg   9%

- Total Carbohydrate 5.1g   2%

- Dietary Fiber 1.7g   7%

- Sugars 1.2g

- Protein 10g   20%

- Vitamin A 133.5µg   9%

- Vitamin C 7.3mg   12%

CAP'N CRUNCH CEREAL CHAFFLE CAKE

PREPARATION TIME: 5 minutes

COOKING TIME: 5 minutes

TOTAL TIME: 10 minutes

SERVINGS: 2

INGREDIENTS

- 1 egg
- 2 tablespoons almond flour
- 1/2 teaspoon coconut flower
- 1 tablespoon butter
- 1 tablespoon cream cheese
- Captain cereal flavor 20 drop
- 1/4 teaspoon vanilla essence
- 1/4 teaspoon baking powder
- 1 tablespoon confectionery
- 1/8 teaspoon xanthan gum
-

PREPARATIONS

1. Preheat mini waffle maker.

2. Mix all ingredients until smooth and

creamy.

3. Add 2-3 tablespoons of batter to the waffle maker and cook for about 2 1/2 minutes.

4. Topped with fresh whipped cream (10 drops of captain cereal flavor and syrup !?

NUTRITIONAL VALUE

- Calories   154
- Total Fat 11.2g 17%
- Cholesterol 113.3mg   38%
- Sodium 96.9mg   4%
- Total Carbohydrate 5.9g   2%
- Dietary Fiber 1.7g   7%
- Sugars 2.7g
- Protein 4.6g   9%
- Vitamin A 104µg   7%

- Vitamin C 0mg   0%

CHOCOLATE CHIP COOKIE CHAFFLE CAKE

PREPARATION TIME: 10 minutes

COOKING TIME: 5 minutes

TOTAL TIME: 15 minutes

SERVINGS: 2

INGREDIENTS

Cake layer ingredients:

- 1 T butter melted
- 1 T Golden Monk Fruit Sweetener
- 1 egg yolk
- 1/8 tsp vanilla essence
- 1/8 teaspoon cake batter extract
- 3 T almond flour
- 1/8 teaspoon baking powder
- 1 T Chocolate Chip Sugar-Free

Whipping cream frosting ingredients:

- 1 teaspoon unflavored gelatin
- 4 tsp cold water
- 1 cup HWC
- 2 T sweetener

PREPARATION

1. Chocolate chip cookie chaff cake recipe description

2. Cake description

3. Mix everything and cook on mini waffle iron for 4 minutes. Repeat for each layer. I decided to make three.

4. Whipping cream frosting procedure

5. Sprinkle gelatin on cold water in a microwave-compatible bowl. Stir and "bloom". This takes about 5 minutes.

6. Microwave the gelatin mixture for 10 seconds. It becomes liquid. Stir to make sure everything is melted.

7. In a chilled mixing bowl, start whipping the cream at low speed. Add the confectionery sugar.

8. Move faster and observe that good peaks begin to form.

9. When the whipped cream has peaked, switch to low speed and squirt the melted liquid gelatin mixture slowly. Once in, switch to high speed and continue tapping until a hard peak is reached.

Note

This recipe uses only half of the whipped cream.

NUTRITIONAL VALUE

- Calories   84
- Total Fat 4.5g 7%
- Cholesterol 71.3mg   24%
- Sodium 122.3mg   5%
- Total Carbohydrate 5.3g   2%
- Dietary Fiber 0.9g   4%
- Sugars 2.1g
- Protein 6.1g   12%

- Vitamin A 298.3µg   20%
- Vitamin C 3.9mg   6%

KETO RED VELVET WAFFLE CAKE

PREPARATION TIME: 10 minutes

COOKING TIME: 5 minutes

TOTAL TIME: 15 minutes

SERVINGS: 2

INGREDIENTS

- 2 Tbs Dutch-processed cocoa
- 2 Tbs Monkfruit Confectioner's
- 1 egg
- 2 drops of optional super drop food coloring
- 1/4 teaspoon baking powder
- 1 Tbs Heavy Whipped Cream
- Frosted ingredients

- 2 Tbs Monkfruit Confectioners

- 2 Tbs cream cheese softens, room temperature

- 1/4 teaspoon transparent vanilla

PREPARATION

1. Put the eggs in a small bowl.

2. Add the ingredients and mix well until smooth and creamy.

3. Put half of the butter in a mini waffle pan and cook for 2 1/2 to 3 minutes until completely cooked.

4. Put the sweetener, cream cheese and vanilla in separate small pots. Mix the frosting until everything mixes well.

5. When the waffle cake has completely cooled to room temperature, spread the frosting.

6. Report makes two mini waffles

NUTRITIONAL VALUE

- Calories   75

- Total Fat 5.8g 9%

- Cholesterol 101.5mg   34%
- Sodium 39.8mg   2%
- Total Carbohydrate 4.1g   1%
- Dietary Fiber 2g   8%
- Sugars 0.4g
- Protein 4.4g   9%
- Vitamin A 70.8μg   5%
- Vitamin C 0mg   0%

BUFFALO CHICKEN CHAFFLE

PREPARATION TIME: 5 minutes

COOKING TIME: 5 minutes

TOTAL TIME: 10 minutes

SERVINGS: 3

INGREDIENTS

PREPARATIONS

NUTRITIONAL VALUE

KETO SMORE'S

PREPARATION TIME: 5 minutes

COOKING TIME: 8 minutes

TOTAL TIME: 13 minutes

SERVINGS: 2

INGREDIENTS

- One large egg
- ½c. Mozzarella shredded
- 1/2 teaspoon of vanilla essence
- 2 tbs swab brown
- ½tbs plantain shell powder
- 1/4 teaspoon baking powder
- Pinch of pink salt
- 2 tbs keto marshmallow cream fluff recipe

PREPARATIONS

1. Make a batch of keto marshmallow cream fluff.
2. Whisk the eggs until creamy.
3. Add vanilla and swirl brown and mix well.
4. Mix the shredded cheese and mix.

5. Next, add psyllium husk powder, baking powder and salt.

6. Mix until well mixed and let the dough rest for 3-4 minutes

7. Prepare/connect waffle maker to preheat.

8. Spread 1/2 batter to the waffle maker and cook for 3-4 minutes

9. Remove and install the cooling rack.

10. Cook the other half of the dough in the same way, remove and let cool.

11. Once cool, assemble the shuffle with marshmallow fluff and chocolate.

12. Use 2 tablespoons marshmallow and bar release chocolate.

13. Eat as it is or toasts the melted and sticky small sandwich!

NUTRITIONAL VALUE

- Calories   120
- Total Fat 8.1g 12%
- Cholesterol 111.2mg   37%

- Sodium 1352.5mg   56%
- Total Carbohydrate 3.1g   1%
- Dietary Fiber 0.2g   1%
- Sugars 0.7g
- Protein 8.3g   17%
- Vitamin A 94.6μg   6%
- Vitamin C 0mg   0%

KETO HASH BROWN CHAFFLE

PREPARATION TIME: 5 minutes

COOKING TIME: 5 minutes

TOTAL TIME: 10 minutes

SERVINGS: 3

INGREDIENTS

PREPARATIONS

NUTRITIONAL VALUE

BACON CHEDDAR BAY BISCUITS CHAFFLE

PREPARATION TIME: 5 minutes

COOKING TIME: 5 minutes

TOTAL TIME: 10 minutes

SERVINGS: 3

INGREDIENTS

PREPARATIONS

NUTRITIONAL VALUE

LOW CARB WAFFLE BOWL

PREPARATION TIME: 5 minutes

COOKING TIME: 5 minutes

TOTAL TIME: 10 minutes

SERVINGS: 1

INGREDIENTS

- One egg. whip

- 1 scoop ketological meal chocolate

- 1 tablespoon almond flour

- 1/4 teaspoon baking powder

PREPARATIONS

1. Preheat the bowl waffle maker and spray with a non-stick cooking spray.

2. Break the eggs in a small bowl. Peel the eggs.

3. Add ketology meal, almond flour and baking powder.

4. Mix until the ingredients are completely together.

5. Place the ingredients in a pre-heated bowl waffle maker for about one to one and a half minutes. When you see the steam

coming out of the machine, you know it's almost done.

6. Use the tongs to remove the hot waffle bowl from the manufacturer.

7. Cool down and have fun!

Note

Use the tongs to remove the hot waffle bowl from the manufacturer.

NUTRITIONAL VALUE

KRISPY KREME COPYCAT CHAFFLE

PREPARATION TIME: 5 minutes

COOKING TIME: 5 minutes

TOTAL TIME: 10 minutes

SERVINGS: 3

INGREDIENTS

PREPARATIONS

NUTRITIONAL VALUE

JICAMA LOADED BAKED POTATO CHAFFLE RECIPE

PREPARATION TIME: 5 minutes

COOKING TIME: 5 minutes

TOTAL TIME: 10 minutes

SERVINGS: 2

INGREDIENTS

- 1 big jicama root
- 1/2 onion minced
- 3 garlic cloves pressed
- 1 cup cheese
- 2 eggs whisked
- salt and pepper

84

PREPARATIONS

1. Put jicama shredded in a large colander, sprinkle with 1-2 tsp of salt. Mix well and drain well.

2. Microwave for 5-8 minutes Mix all ingredients Sprinkle a little cheese on waffle iron before adding 3 T of the mixture, sprinkle a little more cheese on top of the Cook mixture for 5 minutes. Two more flips and fry.

3. Top with a dollop of sour cream, pieces of bacon, cheese and peppers!

NUTRITIONAL VALUE

- Calories   168
- Total Fat 11.8g18%
- Cholesterol 121mg   40%
- Sodium 221.8mg   9%
- Total Carbohydrate 5.1g   2%
- Dietary Fiber 1.7g   7%
- Sugars 1.2g

- Protein 10g   20%

- Vitamin A 133.5µg   9%

- Vitamin C 7.3mg   12%

FRIED PICKLE CHAFFLE STICKS

PREPARATION TIME: 5 minutes

COOKING TIME: 5 minutes

TOTAL TIME: 10 minutes

SERVINGS: 2

INGREDIENTS

- 1 egg

- 1/4 cup pork punk

- 1/2 cup mozzarella cheese

- 1 tablespoon of pickle juice

- 6-8 thin pickled slices

PREPARATIONS

1. Mix together.

2. Add a thin layer to the waffle iron.

3. Suction excess juice from pickles.

4. Add the pickle slices and then mix another thin layer.

5. Cook for 4 minutes.

Note

Immersion sauce: ranch dressing mixed with frank hot sauce

NUTRITIONAL VALUE

- Calories   465
- Total Fat 22.7g   35%
- Cholesterol 250.1mg 83%
- Sodium 1863.2mg   78%
- Total Carbohydrate 3.3g   1%
- Dietary Fiber 1.4g   6%
- Sugars 1.5g
- Protein 59.2g 118%
- Vitamin A 161.1µg   11%

- Vitamin C 1.2mg   2%

WAFFLE IRON TONGS

PREPARATION TIME: 5 minutes

COOKING TIME: 5 minutes

TOTAL TIME: 10 minutes

SERVINGS: 3

INGREDIENTS

PREPARATIONS

NUTRITIONAL VALUE

OREO COOKIE CHAFFLE

PREPARATION TIME: 5 minutes

COOKING TIME: 5 minutes

TOTAL TIME: 10 minutes

SERVINGS: 3

INGREDIENTS

Shuffle ingredients:

- 1 egg

- 1 cup of black cocoa

- 1 tbs monk fruit confectioners blend or favorite keto-approved sweetener

- 1/4 teaspoon baking powder

- Cream cheese 2 room temperature, softened at room temperature

- 1 tablespoon of mayonnaise

- 1/4 teaspoon non-liquid instant coffee powder

- Pinch salt

- 1 teaspoon of vanilla

Matting ingredient:

- 2 Tbs monk fruit confectionery

- 2 Tbs cream cheese softens, room temperature

- 1/4 teaspoon transparent vanilla

PREPARATIONS

1. Add other ingredients and mix well until smooth and creamy.

2. Divide the batter into 3 and pour each into a mini waffle maker and cook until it is fully cooked for 2 1/2 to 3 minutes.

3. Add the sweetener, cream cheese, and vanilla in a separate small bowl. Mix the frosting until all is well embedded.

4. Spread the frosting after it has cooled down to room temperature.

NUTRITIONAL VALUE

- Calories   69
- Total Fat 5g   8%
- Cholesterol 67.4mg   22%
- Sodium 874.7mg   36%
- Total Carbohydrate 2.7g   1%
- Dietary Fiber 0.7g   3%
- Sugars 0.9g
- Protein 3.5g   7%
- Vitamin A 42.9μg   3%
- Vitamin C 0mg   0%

CORNDOG CHAFFLE

PREPARATION TIME: 5 minutes

COOKING TIME: 5 minutes

TOTAL TIME: 10 minutes

SERVINGS: 3

INGREDIENTS

- Mix flax egg-1 T ground flaxseed with 3 T water
- If you are not allergic to egg whites, skip flax and

use one large egg

- 1 1/2 T melted butter

- 2 teaspoons sweetener

- 3 T almond flour

- 1/4 teaspoon baking powder

- 1 egg yolk

- 2 T heap Mexican blended cheese

- 1 T chopped jalapeno

- 15-20 drop cornbread flavor

- Extra cheese to sprinkle on a waffle maker

PREPARATIONS

1. Mix everything together. Rest for 5 minutes. If too thick, add 1 T water or HWC.

2. Sprinkle the shredded cheese on the bottom of the waffle maker. Add 1/3 of the batter. Sprinkle the shredded cheese

on top. Close the waffle iron. Do not press. If the cheese is crispy, remove it. Repeat. Make 3

3. Note

4. This is the cornbread flavor I used.

5. Corn Silk (Zea Mays) Glycerite, Organic Dry Silk Alcohol-Free Liquid Extract 2 oz

BEST KETO SHUFFLE

PREPARATION TIME: 10 minutes

COOKING TIME: 5 minutes

TOTAL TIME: 15 minutes

SERVINGS: 4

INGREDIENTS

- 2 eggs

- 1 cup shredded cheddar cheese

- 1 Scoop Perfect Keto Flavored Collagen

PREPARATIONS

1. Heat the mini waffle iron.

2. Mix all ingredients in a medium-sized bowl.

3. Spoon 1/4 cup of mix into waffle maker and cook for 3-4 minutes or until waffles is crisp.

4. Serve and enjoy!

NUTRITIONAL VALUE

- Calories: 326

- Fat: 24.75g

- Carbohydrates: 2g (net: 1g)

- Fiber: 1g

- Protein: 25g

CRISPY EVERYTHING BAGEL CHAFFLE

PREPARATION TIME: 8 minutes

COOKING TIME: 5 minutes

TOTAL TIME: 13 minutes

SERVINGS: 2

INGREDIENTS

- 3 Tbs Parmesan Cheese shredded

- 1 tsp Everything Bagel Seasoning

PREPARATIONS

1. Preheat mini waffle maker.

2. Place the griddle with the Parmesan cheese and whisk. About 3 minutes. Please leave it long enough, or let it cool

down when it cools down. An important step forward!

3. Sprinkle a teaspoon of Everything Bagel Seasoning over the melted cheese. Once heated, leave the waffle iron open!

4. Unplug the mini waffle maker and urge to cool for a few minutes. This allows the cheese to cool sufficiently to combine and crisp.

5. After cooling for about 2 minutes, it is still dry.

6. Peel warm with a mini spatula (do not use hot cheese in a mini waffle iron; cool completely for crisp chips! These chips pack a powerful crunch that you often miss in keto Note: The more cheese you use, the thicker the chips, the less cheese you use, the lighter and crisper the chips!

EVERYTHING CHAFFLE

PREPARATION TIME: 8 minutes

COOKING TIME: 10 minutes

TOTAL TIME: 18 minutes

SERVINGS: 2

INGREDIENTS:

- 1 Large Egg
- 1 Ounce 6 Cheese Italian Blend Cheese, Finely Shredded
- 3 Tablespoons Almond Flour
- 1 Pinch Salt
- Butter Flavored Non-Stick Cooking Spray

Topping

- 2 Ounces Cream Cheese
- 2 Teaspoons Everything Bagel Seasoning

PREPARATION

1. Plug in the mini waffle maker and preheat it. There is a light for many waffle makers to indicate when it is preheated. Be sure that it is completely heated before

continuing for the best results.

2. Crack the large egg into a small bowl and beat vigorously with a fork until well-mixed yolk and white.

3. Chop the shredded Italian cheese into smaller pieces using a small chopping board and medium-sized knife. It ensures that the cheese can be distributed more evenly throughout the egg mixture.

4. Add the egg mixture with the butter, almond flour and salt and whisk with a fork until all is well mixed.

5. Sprinkle waffle maker with non-stick cooking spray flavored with butter.

6. Put 1/2 of the mixture in a miniature waffle maker's grill center. Stretch the mixture to the grill edges and close the waffle maker.

7. Cook the chaffle for 5 minutes or brown

and cook through until toasty.

8. Gently remove the chaffle using a small fork and place it to cool on a sheet of paper towels.

9. Spray waffle maker with non-stick cooking spray flavored with butter and cook the remaining mixture of the chaffle the same as the first.

10. When they cool down, chaffles will become crisper.

11. Layer cream cheese chaffles and sprinkle with bagel seasoning.

NUTRITIONAL VALUE

Calories: 249kcal | Carbohydrates: 5g | Protein: 11g | Fat: 22g | Saturated Fat: 7g | Cholesterol: 116mg | Sodium: 169mg | Potassium: 91mg | Fiber: 2g | Sugar: 1g | Iron: 1mg

PUMPKIN CHAFFLE KETO SUGAR COOKIES

PREPARATION TIME: 10 minutes

COOKING TIME: 5 minutes

TOTAL TIME: 15 minutes

SERVINGS: 2

INGREDIENTS

FOR KETO SUGAR COOKIES

- 1 T butter melted

- 1 T sweetener

- 1 egg yolk

- 1/8 tsp vanilla essence

- 1/8 teaspoon cake batter extract

- 3Tbs almond flour

- 1/8 teaspoon baking powder

- Icing ingredients

- 1 T sweetener

- 1/4 teaspoon of vanilla essence

- 1-2 teaspoons of water
- Sprinkle ingredients

PREPARATION

1. Stir all ingredients together. Rest for 5 minutes
2. Stir again.
3. Refrigerate for 15 minutes.
4. Cook for 4 minutes.
5. Repeat. Let cool.
6. Add icing and sprinkles as needed.

APPLE PIE CHURRO CHAFFLE TACOS

PREPARATION TIME: 30 minutes

COOKING TIME: 30 minutes

TOTAL TIME: 60 minutes

SERVINGS: 2

INGREDIENTS:

Chayote apple pie filling

- 1 chayote squash cook, peel, slice
- 1 T Kerrygold butter melted
- 2 packets True Lemon
- 1/8 tsp tartar cream
- 1/4 cup swallow brown
- 2 tsp Ceylon cinnamon powder
- 1/8 teaspoon ginger powder
- 1/8 teaspoon nutmeg

Cinnamon shuffle

- 2 eggs room temperature
- 1/4 cup mozzarella cheese shredded
- 1 tsp Ceylon cinnamon
- 1 T confectionery
- Coconut flower 2 tsp
- 1/8 teaspoon baking powder
- 1 teaspoon of vanilla essence

PREPARATIONS

1. Blend all ingredients together and mix well in the chayote.

2. Place the mixture in a shallow baking dish and cover with foil. Bake for about 20 minutes.

3. Place 1/4 of the mixture in a food processor or small blender and heat until the consistency of the apple sauce is achieved.

4. Apply the slices to the chayote and mix.

5. Mix shells.

6. Add some sweetener, cinnamon and vanilla.

7. Mix well, guy.

8. Add the remaining ingredients and stir well.

9. Place 3T of the battery in the preheated Dash Mini Griddle.

10. Cook for five minutes.

11. Sprinkle with cinnamon and granular sweetener mixture.

12. To mount, place the chaffles in the taco holders or fold softly to shape.

13. Apply 1/4 of the apple filling to each taco cover.

14. Finish with ice cream or vanilla bean.

KETO CHAFFLE CHURRO

PREPARATION TIME: 10 minutes

COOKING TIME: 4 minutes

TOTAL TIME: 14 minutes

SERVINGS: 2

INGREDIENTS:

- 1 egg

- 1/2 cup mozzarella cheese shredded

- 2 tbsp swallow brown sweetener

- 1/2 tsp cinnamon

PREPARATION

1. Preheat the mini waffle of iron.

2. Whip the egg in a small bowl.

3. Apply the shredded cheese to the combination of eggs.

4. Place half of the egg mixture in a mini waffle pan and cook until golden brown. While the mini Chaffle is cooking, add the Swerve Brown Sweetener and cinnamon in a separate small bowl.

5. Once the Chaffle is done, cut it into slices.

NUTRITIONAL VALUE

- Calories   76
- Total Fat 4.3g 7%
- Cholesterol 14mg   5%
- Sodium 147.5mg   6%
- Total Carbohydrate 4.1g   1%
- Dietary Fiber 1.2g   5%
- Sugars 1.9g

- Protein 5.5g   11%

- Vitamin A 55µg   4%

- Vitamin C 0.9mg   2%

KETO "APPLE" FRITTER CHAFFLES

PREPARATION TIME: 30 minutes

COOKING TIME: 30 minutes

TOTAL TIME: 60 minutes

SERVINGS: 5

INGREDIENTS

"APPLE" FRITTER FILLING INGREDIENTS

- 2 cups of diced jicama

- 1/4 cup and 1 tablespoon Swerve sweetener blend

- 4 tbsp butter

- 1 teaspoon cinnamon

- 1/8 teaspoon of nutmeg

- Dash clove

- 1/2 teaspoon vanilla

- Lorann Oils Apple Flavor 20 Drops

Ingredients for shuffle

- 2 eggs

- 1/2 cup of grated mozzarella cheese

- 1 tablespoon almond flour

- 1 tsp coconut flour

- 1/2 teaspoon baking powder

Glaze drug ingredients

- 1 tablespoon butter

- 2 tsp heavy cream

- 3 cups of powdered sweetener such as Swerve Confectioners

- 1/4 teaspoon vanilla essence

PREPARATION VALUE

1. Keto "Berry" Fritter Filling

2. Cut the jicama and cut into small dice.

3. In a medium-low heat pan, melt the butter and add the diced jicama and the sweetener.

4. Lave it to slowly simmer for 10-20 minutes, looking at it till the jicama is tender, stirring frequently. Avoid using high heat, or the sweetener will easily caramelize and burn. A light amber color should grow and thicken.

5. When the jicama is tender, remove from heat and stir in the spices and flavourings.

6. Keto "Apple" Fritter Chaffle

7. Preheat up to hot waffle iron.

8. Beat all ingredients, except milk, in a medium bowl. Stir the mixture of jicama into the eggs.

9. Put 1 tablespoon of grated cheese on that waffle iron.

10. Spoon 2 tablespoons of the egg/jicama mixture into the waffle iron and finish with another tablespoon of the milk.

11. Open the waffle and cook for 5-7 minutes until well browned and crispy.

12. Remove from the wire rack.

13. Repeat it 3-4 times.

14. Keto "Apple" Fritter Chiffle Icing

15. Melt butter in a small saucepan and add Swerve and heavy cream.

16. Simmer over an average heat for few minutes or until lightly thickened.

17. Stir the vanilla.

18. Drizzle the hot frost over the cuffs. It's going to harden as it cools.

NUTRITIONAL VALUE

- Calories   186
- Total Fat 14.3g   22%
- Cholesterol 108.1mg 36%
- Sodium 117.7mg   5%

- Total Carbohydrate 8.5g   3%
- Dietary Fiber 3.4g   13%
- Sugars 1.5g
- Protein 7g   14%
- Vitamin A 148.2μg   10%
- Vitamin C 10.5mg   18%

GRAIN-FREE, LOW CARB KETO WAFFLES

PREPARATION TIME: 5 minutes

COOKING TIME: 15 minutes

TOTAL TIME: 20 minutes

SERVINGS: 2

INGREDIENTS

- 1 tablespoon almond flour

- 1 egg

- 1 tsp vanilla

- Cinnamon 1 shake

- 1 teaspoon baking powder

- 1 cup mozzarella cheese (full fat, defatted or defatted is effective, depending on preference)

PREPARATIONS

1. In a bowl, mix the egg and vanilla extract.

2. Mix baking powder, almond flour and cinnamon.

3. Finally, add mozzarella cheese and coat evenly with the mixture.

4. Spray the waffle maker with oil and heat to the highest setting.

5. Cook the waffles and check every 5 minutes until crunchy and golden. Tip: Put half of the batter. Waffle makers can overflow, making it a cumbersome process. We recommend putting a sylpat mat for easy cleaning.

6. Carefully remove and place over butter and your choice of low carbohydrate syrup.

Note

Need a waffle maker? There are several options!

If you need the more sweetness, you can add a sweetener such as Swerve. I did not choose and instead used a low carb syrup that I felt sweet enough.

After cooling for 1 minute, the crunch returns immediately. In fact, it is crisp than fresh. This seems like a miracle for me.

Note that when frozen, the mozzarella flavor

actually increases. Before you eat it, add a small amount of cinnamon and a teaspoon of butter on top. It is best to enjoy it fresh.

These can be preserved for 7 days in an air-free Ziplock bag.

As shown by the user, this recipe creates four mini-chaffles with the DASH mini-waffle maker or two shuffles with the regular-size waffle maker. Eat something that matches the macro. However, the nutrition information listed is for one large chaffle and is for one serving.

Macros vary by component. The use of full fat, skim, or defatted cheese may increase or decrease nutritional information. This recipe uses defatted cheese, so be sure to recalculate your macros if you follow closely.

NUTRITIONAL VALUE

- Calories   150
- Total Fat 9g   14%
- Cholesterol 113mg   38%
- Sodium 250.3mg 10%
- Total Carbohydrate 6.5g 2%
- Dietary Fiber 0.9g   4%
- Sugars 0.5g
- Protein 10.7g   21%
- Vitamin A 40.2µg   3%
- Vitamin C 0mg   0%

KETO CHAFFLE TACOS

PREPARATION TIME: 5 minutes

COOKING TIME: 5 minutes

TOTAL TIME: 10 minutes

SERVINGS: 2

INGREDIENTS

- 1/2 cup cheese cheddar or mozzarella cheese,

shredded

- 1 egg

- 1/4 teaspoon Italian seasoning

- 1 pound ground beef octopus seasoning ingredients

- 1 tsp chili powder

- 1 teaspoon cumin

- 1/2 teaspoon garlic powder

- 1/2 teaspoon cocoa powder

- 1/4 teaspoon onion powder

- 1/4 teaspoon salt

- 1/12 teaspoon smoked paprika

Taco meat seasoning for large lots

- 1/4 cup chili powder

- Grand cumin 1/4 cup

- 2 tablespoons of garlic powder

- 2 tablespoons cocoa powder

- 1 tablespoon onion powder

- 1 tablespoon

- 1 teaspoon smoked paprika

PREPARATIONS

1. Cook minced meat or minced meat first.

2. Add all taco meat seasonings. Cocoa powder is optional, but completely enhances the flavor of all other seasonings!

3. While making octopus meat, start making keto chaffles.

4. Preheat the waffle maker. I am using a mini waffle maker.

5. In a small bowl, first whip the eggs.

6. Add shredded cheese and seasonings.

7. Put half shuffle mixture into mini waffle maker and cook for about 3-4 minutes.

8. Cook the second half of the mixture repeatedly to make a second shuffle.

9. Add warm taco meat to octopus chaffle.

10. Topped with lettuce, tomato and cheese and

serve warm!

Note

I tend to create this in large batches, so there are always some at hand! Seal in a mason jar and place in the kitchen pantry. Just add a little label and you're ready to go. There is no real reason to buy a pre-made taco seasoning packet, as making taco seasonings is so easy.

NUTRITIONAL VALUE

KETO ICE CREAM SANDWICH CHAFFLE

PREPARATION TIME: 5 minutes

COOKING TIME: 5 minutes

TOTAL TIME: 10 minutes

SERVINGS: 2

INGREDIENTS

- 2 Tbs cocoa

- 2 Tbs Monkfruit Confectioner's

- 1 egg

- 1/4 teaspoon baking powder

- 1 Tbs Heavy Whipped Cream

- Add selected keto ice cream

PREPARATION

1. Whip the egg in a small bowl.

2. Pour half of tbatter into the waffle maker and cook until fully cooked for 2 1/2 to 3 minutes.

3. Allow the ice cream to cool completely before the ice cream is placed in the center.

4. Freeze all the way to solid.

5. Serve and bear the weather!

KETO CHOCOLATE TWINKIE COPYCAT CHAFFLE

PREPARATION TIME: 5 minutes

COOKING TIME: 12 minutes

TOTAL TIME: 17 minutes

SERVINGS: 3

INGREDIENTS

- 2 tablespoons of butter (cooled)
- 2 oz cream cheese softened
- Two large egg room temperature
- 1 teaspoon of vanilla essence
- 1/4 cup Lacanto confectionery
- Pinch of pink salt
- 1/4 cup almond flour
- 2 tablespoons coconut powder
- 2 tablespoons cocoa powder
- 1 teaspoon baking powder

PREPARATIONS

1. Preheat the Maker of Corndog.
2. Melt the butter for a minute and let it cool.
3. In the butter, whisk the eggs until smooth.
4. Remove sugar, cinnamon, sweetener and blend well.

5. Add flour of almond, flour of coconut, powder of cacao and baking powder.

6. Blend until well embedded.

7. Fill each well with ~2 tablespoons of batter and spread evenly.

8. Lift from the rack and cool it down.

NUTRITIONAL VALUE

- Calories   104

- Total Fat 6.2g 10%

- Cholesterol 67.1mg   22%

- Sodium 485.5mg   20%

- Total Carbohydrate 5.3g   2%

- Dietary Fiber 1.7g   7%

- Sugars 1.6g

- Protein 4.4g   9%

- Vitamin A 80.1µg   5%

- Vitamin C 0mg   0%

KETO SAUSAGE BALL CHAFFLE

PREPARATION TIME: 5 minutes

COOKING TIME: 3 minutes

TOTAL TIME: 8 minutes

SERVINGS: 2

INGREDIENTS

- 1 pound bulk Italian sausage

- 1 cup almond flour

- 2 teaspoons baking powder

- 1 cup shredded cheddar cheese

- 1/4 cup grated parmesan cheese

- 1 egg, or if you are allergic to eggs, you can use flax eggs

PREPARATIONS

1. Heat the maker of mini waffles to average.

2. Put all the ingredients in a big bowl and combine well by hand.

3. Place a paper plate to trap any drops under the waffle maker.

4. In a hot waffle maker, spoon a 3 T blend.

5. Cook for a total of 3 minutes. Switch over and cook to get a crisp look for another 2 minutes.

NUTRITIONAL VALUE

KETO CHAFFLE STUFFING

PREPARATION TIME: 20 minutes

COOKING TIME: 40 minutes

TOTAL TIME: 60 minutes

SERVINGS: 4

INGREDIENTS

Basic shuffle ingredients

- 1/2 cup cheese mozzarella, cheddar cheese, or a

combination of both

- 2 eggs

- 1/4 teaspoon of garlic powder

- 1/2 teaspoon onion powder

- 1/2 teaspoon dried chicken seasoning

- 1/4 teaspoon salt

- 1/4 teaspoon pepper

Ingredients for filling

- 1 diced onion

- 2 celery stems

- 4 oz mushrooms diced

- 4 cups of butter for sauteing

- 3 eggs

PREPARATIONS

1. First, make a shuffle. This recipe makes four mini-chaffles.

2. Preheat mini waffle iron.

3. Preheat oven to 350F

4. In a medium bowl, mix the shuffle

125

ingredients.

5. Pour 1/4 of the mixture into a mini waffle maker and cook each chaffle for about 4 minutes each.

6. When they are all cooked, set aside.

7. In a small skillet, fry the onions, celery and mushrooms until soft.

8. In a separate bowl, split the shuffle into small pieces and add sauteed vegetables and three eggs. Mix until the ingredients are completely bonded.

9. Add the mixture of fillings to a small casserole dish (about 4x4) and bake at 350 degrees for about 30-40 minutes.

Note

(Make four shuffles)

NUTRITIONAL VALUE

- Calories   229
- % Daily Value*
- Total Fat 17.6g27%
- Cholesterol 265.6mg   89%
- Sodium 350mg   15%
- Total Carbohydrate 4.6g   2%
- Dietary Fiber 1.1g   5%
- Sugars 2g
- Protein 13.7g   27%
- Vitamin A 217.2µg   14%
- Vitamin C 2.4mg   4%

KETO BLUEBERRY CHAFFLE

PREPARATION TIME: 5 minutes

COOKING TIME: 15 minutes

TOTAL TIME: 20 minutes

SERVINGS: 5

INGREDIENTS

- 1 cup mozzarella cheese

- 2 tablespoons almond flour

- 1 tsp baking powder

- 2 eggs

- 1 tsp cinnamon

- Sweetener 2 tsp

- 3 tablespoons blueberry

PREPARATIONS

1. Heat up your waffle maker Dash mini.

2. Place mozzarella cheese, almond flour, baking powder, milk, cinnamon, and blueberries in a mixing bowl. Blend well in order to blend all the ingredients together.

3. Spray the non-stick cooking spray on your mini waffle maker.

4. Attach a cup of blueberry keto waffle

batter in a little less than 1/4.

5. Close the lid and cook 3-5 minutes of the chaffle. Check to see if it's crispy and golden at the 3-minute mark. If it is not or if it sticks to the top of the waffle cooker, close the lid and cook for 1-2 more minutes.

6. Serve with a drop of sugar or keto syrup from swerve confectioners.

7. Notes Net carbs-2 g net carbs per chaffle of blueberry

NUTRITIONAL VALUE

Calories: 116kcal | Carbohydrates: 3g | Protein: 8g | Fat: 8g | Saturated Fat: 4g | Cholesterol: 83mg | Sodium: 166mg | Potassium: 142mg | Fiber: 1g | Vitamin C: 1mg | Calcium: 177mg | Iron: 1mg

KETO CHAFFLE BREAKFAST SANDWICH

PREPARATION TIME: 10 minutes

COOKING TIME: 10 minutes

TOTAL TIME: 20 minutes

SERVINGS: 6

INGREDIENTS

- Two large eggs, split

- 1/2 cup of minced mozzarella or hard cheese

- 2 slice bacon (60 g / 2.1 oz)

- 1 slice of tomato (27 g / 1 oz)

- Sliced cheese such as cheddar cheese (28 g / 1 oz)

PREPARATIONS

1. Preheat mini waffle iron. Whisk one of the eggs in a small bowl. If necessary, add almond flour and mix well. If only eggs are used, the dough will be very smooth.

2. Sprinkle a quarter of the minced mozzarella cheese (about 1/2 oz / 14 g) on a waffle iron and sprinkle half of the whipped egg on top. Alternatively, whisk eggs directly with mozzarella cheese. Keto chaffle breakfast sandwich

3. Sprinkle mozzarella a quarter more (about 1/2 oz / 14 g) and close the iron. Cook for 2-3 minutes until the waffles come off easily. Repeat for the second waffle.

4. Keto shuffle breakfast sandwich

5. Cook the bacon slices in a small skillet and scramble the remaining eggs in the same skillet. Keto chaffle breakfast sandwich

6. Waffles on top of sliced cheese, tomatoes, bacon and eggs, Finish with another waffle and serve.

NUTRITIONAL VALUE

- Calories from carbs 4%,

- protein 28%, fat 68%

- Total carbs5.8 grams

- Fiber0.3 grams

- Sugars2.3 grams

- saturated fat19.8 grams

- Sodium1,194 mg(52% RDA)

- Magnesium47 mg(12% RDA)

- Potassium455 mg(23% EMR)

KETO CORNBREAD CHAFFLE

PREPARATION TIME: 5 minutes

COOKING TIME: 5 minutes

TOTAL TIME: 10 minutes

SERVINGS: 2

INGREDIENTS

- 1 egg

-

- 5 slice Jalapeno option-freshly picked or fresh

- 1 teaspoon of Frank's Red Hot Sauce

- 1/4 teaspoon corn extract is an essential secret ingredient!

- Pinch of salt

PREPARATIONS

1. Mini waffle makers preheating placing the eggs in a small bowl

2. The remaining ingredients are added and combined until well absorbed.

3. Apply 1 tablespoon shredded cheese to the waffle maker for 30 seconds before removing the mixture. It produces a very clean and friendly crust!

4. To a preheated waffle maker, add half of the mixture.

5. Cook for a total of 3-4 minutes. The more you're eating, the crunchier.

6. Enjoy it served warm!

NUTRITIONAL VALUE

- Calories 150
- % Daily Value*
- Total Fat 11.8g 18%
- Cholesterol 121mg   40%
- Sodium 1399.4mg   58%
- Total Carbohydrate 1.1g   0%
- Dietary Fiber 0g   0%
- Sugars 0.2g
- Protein 9.6g   19%
- Vitamin A 134.1µg   9%
- Vitamin C 0.1mg   0%

BASIC CHAFFLE

BASIC CHAFFLE RECIPE

PREPARATION TIME: 1 minute

COOKING TIME: 6 minutes

TOTAL TIME: 7 minutes

SERVINGS: 2

INGREDIENTS

- One large egg

- 1/2 cup mozzarella cheese finely chopped

PREPARATIONS

1. Connect a waffle maker and heat.

2. Break the eggs into small bowls and beat with a fork. Add mozzarella cheese and mix.

3. Spray the non-stick spray on the waffle iron.

4. Pour half of the egg mixture into a heated waffle iron and cook for 2-3 minutes.

5. Carefully remove the waffle and cook the remaining dough.

6. Serve warm with butter and sugar-free

syrup.

Note

Try adding a little vanilla or cinnamon for the next level of breakfast chaffle!

NUTRITIONAL VALUE

CALORIES: 202 TOTAL FAT: 13g SATURATED FAT: 6g TRANS FAT: 0g UNSATURATED FAT: 5g CHOLESTEROL: 214mg SODIUM: 364mg CARBOHYDRATES: 3g NET CARBOHYDRATES: 3g FIBER: 0g SUGAR: 1g SUGAR ALCOHOLS: 0g PROTEIN: 16g

KETO CHAFFLE STUFFING CHAFFLE

PREPARATION TIME: 10 minutes

COOKING TIME: 65 minutes

TOTAL TIME: 75 minutes

SERVINGS: 8

INGREDIENTS

- 4 eggs
- 2 cups of mozzarella cheese
- 1/2 cup of almond flour
- 1/4 cup of parmesan cheese
- 1 teaspoon of baking powder
- 1 teaspoon of salt
- 1/4 cup of olive oil
- 2 tablespoon of parmesan cheese
- 1/4 teaspoon of garlic powder

  STUFFING INGREDIENTS

- 1 small leek or onion
- 8 ounces of champignons
- 1 tablespoon of herb

PREPARATION

1. 1/4 cup Whisk together all the ingredients

of the chaffle-egg, mozzarella cheese, almond flour, parmesan cheese, salt and baking powder.

2. Pour 1/4 of the chaffle mixture into the middle of the waffle iron in a bowl.

3. Remove the chaffle and repeat with the remaining batter until four chaffles are in place. Cut the chaffles into small chunks or bite-size.

4. Place the pieces of the chaffle in a large bowl. Add olive oil, 2 teaspoons of parmesan cheese, 1/4 teaspoon of garlic and 1/4 teaspoon of black pepper. When mixed, shake or shake.

5. Place powdered chaffle pieces on a baking tray lined with parchment and bake for 30 minutes at 250 degrees. Remove and set aside from heat. Set the oven up to 350 degrees.

6. While the breading of the chaffle is cooking, move on to make the mushroom mixture of the bacon. Cook bacon over medium-high heat in a larger skillet until crispy. Take pieces of bacon from the pan and set aside, leaving behind the bacon grease.

7. Slices of bacon frying in a pan Lower to medium heat stovetop. Attach the leek sliced and cook for 1 minute.

8. Cooking leek in a pan Remove onions, salt 1/2 teaspoon and black pepper 1/4 teaspoon. Continue to cook until slightly hardened mushrooms.

9. Cooking mushrooms and leeks in a skillet Remove thin sage and cook for 1 minute. Add white wine and continue cooking from the bottom of the skillet while scraping the brown bits. It's got all the spice. Let it take 2 minutes to cook.

10. Wine in the mushroom mixture context Apply chaffle breading to the bottom of a large saucepan

11. Dry breading of the chaffle in a saucepan Spoon mushroom mixture on top of the breading of the chaffle, Cut the broth and parsley from the chicken bone. Remove crumbles of bacon. Drizzle on top of the melted butter. Stir halfway through the filling of the chaffle. If required, add more chicken broth.

KETO CHAFFLE

PREPARATION TIME: 5 minutes

COOKING TIME: 5 minutes

TOTAL TIME: 10 minutes

SERVINGS: 2

INGREDIENTS

- One large egg
- 1/2 c. Shred cheese
- A pinch of salt

- Seasonings

PREPARATIONS

1. Preheat mini waffle maker. (I used this mini waffle maker purchased from Amazon)

2. Whisk eggs in a bowl until whisked.

3. Shred cheese (favorite taste and combination).

4. Add cheese, salt and seasoning to the egg and mix well.

5. Rip half of the mixture in a waffle maker and spread evenly.

6. Cook for 3-4 minutes until liking (crisp).

7. Pull out and let cool.

8. Add the remaining dough and cook the second waffle.

9. Pleasant!

Note

Making: 2 waffle slices

CPSIA information can be obtained
at www.ICGtesting.com
Printed in the USA
BVHW090724180621
609825BV00004B/291